Divine Love
Words of the Mother

Acknowledgements

Although the information provided in this booklet was accurate at the time of publication, Auroville is a place of constant change, and it is possible that certain details may no longer be correct at the time of purchase.

First edition

Copyright : Prisma, Auroville
Author : Franz Fassbender

ISBN 978-93-95460-75-0 (Paperpack)
ISBN 978-93-95460-43-9 (ebook)

BISAC Code:
REL113000, RELIGION / Essays
PHI034000, PHILOSOPHY / Social
PHI015000, PHILOSOPHY / Mind & Body
REL036000, RELIGION / Inspirational
REL062000, RELIGION / Spirituality

Thema Subject Category:
QRVK, Spirituality and religious experience
QRVP, Religious life and practice
VXA, Mind, body, spirit: thought and practice

Cataloging-in-Publication Data for this title is available from the Library of Congress.

Published by:
PRISMA, an imprint of Digital Media Initiatives
PRISMA, Aurelec / Prayogshala,
Auroville 605101, Tamil Nadu, Indiaa
www.prisma.haus

CONTENTS

1. AN OLD CHALDEAN LEGEND — 5
2. THE GREAT SECRET — 11
3. THE HIGHEST SUMMIT OF MANIFESTATION — 17
4. THE PULSATIONS OF LOVE — 27
5. LOVE IS THE PERMANENCE — 35
6. MISSIONED LOVE — 41
7. TRUE LOVE — 53
8. FLOWERS — 63
9. HUMAN LOVE — 71
10. THE DIRECT TRANSFORMING POWER — 91
11. FIRST TRUTH THEN LOVE — 99
12. THE MOMENT HAS COME — 109
13. PREPARATION IS NEEDED — 115
14. EVERYTHING WILL YIELD — 125

Arousing consciousness in things inert,
He imposed upon dark atom and dumb mass
The diamond script of the Imperishable,
Inscribed on the dim heart of fallen things
A paean-song of the free Infinite
And the Name, foundation of eternity,
And traced on the awake exultant cells
In the ideographs of the Ineffable
The lyric of the love that waits through Time
And the mystic volume of the Book of Bliss
And the message of the superconscient Fire.

Savitri, Book II, Canto 8   Sri Aurobindo

An Old Chaldean Legend

Divine Love
A flower that is said to blossom even in the desert.
Punica granatum. Orange red, double

AN OLD CHALDEAN LEGEND

Long ago, very long ago, in the desert land that is now Arabia, a divine being incarnated on earth to awaken it to the Supreme Love. As one would expect, he was persecuted by men, misunderstood, suspected, hunted after. Mortally wounded by his assailants, he wished to die alone, quietly, so that his work might be accomplished; and, pursued by them, he fled. Suddenly in the broad barren plain, a tiny bush of pomegranate appeared. The Saviour stole under its low branches in order to give up his body in peace; and at once the bush expanded miraculously, increased itself, widened, became deep and luxuriant in such a way that when the pursuers passed by they did not even suspect that the One whom they were chasing was hidden there, and they continued on their way.

While, drop by drop, the sacred blood fell, fertilising the soil, the bush covered itself with marvellous flowers, scarlet, enormous – clusters of petals, innumerable drops of blood...

These are the flowers that, for us, express and hold the Divine Love.

14th November 1955

Yesterday morning I distributed petals of "Divine Love". The previous night was, here, the darkest of the year and in India it is a great festival. Its true significance is that the Divine's Love is at the base and core of all manifestation, even where it seems most completely inconscient.

When Consciousness separated from its Origin and became Inconscience, the Origin emanated Love to reawaken Consciousness from the depth of the Inconscience and bring it back into touch with its Origin.

It may be said that at its origin love is the supreme power of attraction which awakens, in response, the irresistible need of an absolute self-giving; they are the two poles of the urge towards complete fusion.

No other movement could, better and more surely than this, throw a bridge across the abyss dug by the sense of separation that comes from the formation of the individual. It was necessary to bring back to itself what had been projected into space without destroying for this purpose the universe created thus.

That is why love sprang up, the irresistible power of union.

When the baker wants to make the dough of his bread rise, he puts some leaven into it, and it is from within that the transformation takes place.

When the Divine wanted to rouse Matter, awaken it and make it rise towards God, He threw Himself into Matter under the form of love, and it is from within that the transformation takes place.

So it is by living from within an organisation that one can help it to become enlightened and rise towards the Truth.

17th January 1965

THE GREAT SECRET

And then they say, 'I want to close my eyes and see nothing but Him. I want nothing more of the outer world.' And they forget there's Love! That is the great Secret, that which is behind the Existent and the Non-Existent, the Personal and the Impersonal – Love. Not a love between two things, two beings ... A love containing everything.

16th May 1960

She brought me a little poem in French on "The Beloved and His Beloved" (all that up above), which, I must say, was very pretty. So she read it to me, and when it was over I told her, "But Love – this Beloved and his Beloved – is not a person, these are not persons; they are not human beings, not even symbolic human beings...." And at that point something opened up above, and I told her what Love is.

She was gripped at the throat so strongly that afterwards I almost lost my voice.

11th October 1967

Whereas "That" is beyond Time and Space. When you have gone from the Creation to Non-creation, which do not follow each other, they are concomitant, if you go beyond, you encounter this "something" which, I don't know why, I call Love.... Probably because the vibration of true Love, what I call divine Love, which is at work in the world, bears the closest resemblance to That. It is something absolutely inexpressible, which belongs neither to "receiving" nor to "giving", neither to uniting nor to absorbing, nothing like all that.... It's something very particular.

(long silence)

I remember, that night I spoke of, I WAS that Pulsation, and each burst of pulsation created. Well, it was the first expression of That in the Manifestation; and it was already in action, it was already in movement. But the Vibration BEHIND that is... I might say the potentiality of everything – of everything that becomes perceptible to us through the Manifestation; because it is everything that in our consciousness gets divided into various possibilities, like truth, love, life, power, etc (but all that is nothing, of course, it's dust in comparison). And it's everything together;

not the union of different things: it's EVERYTHING – everything, and it is absolutely ONE, but everything is there. And That is what one finds beyond the Manifestation and the Non-manifestation – the Manifestation almost looks like child's play in comparison. That Pulsation was the origin of the Manifestation.

And Non-manifestation is blissful Immobility – it's more than that, but it's essentially that: blissful Immobility. It's the supreme and supremely divine essence of rest. And both, Manifestation and Non-manifestation, are together, and they come from That.

20th March 1965

The Highest Summit of Manifestation

This japa, you know, didn't at all come from here (Mother points to her head). *It's something I received fully formed, and to such an extent that I couldn't even change the place of a single thing – a will seemed to oppose any change. It's a long series unfolding according to a law that probably corresponds to what is needed to develop this consciousness and the work it has to do (I suppose – I don't really know and I haven't tried to know). But a sort of law makes it impossible to change the position of even a single word, because these are not words – they are fully formed states of consciousness. And the whole series culminates with: 'Manifest Your Love'. This is the highest summit of the possibility of manifestation.*

12th July 1961

I learned to do the same thing, and with great dexterity; I could halt on any plane, do what I had to do there, move around freely, see, observe, and then speak about what I had seen. And my last stage, which Théon called 'pathétisme', a very barbaric but very expressive word, bordered on the Formless – he sometimes used the Jewish terminology, calling the Supreme 'The Formless'. From this last stage one passed to the Formless – there was no further body to leave behind, one was beyond all possible forms, even all thought forms. In this domain, the last stage before the Formless, one experienced total unity – unity in something that was the essence of Love; Love was a manifestation more... 'dense', he would always say, there were all sorts of different 'densities'; and Love was a denser expression of That, the sense of perfect Unity – perfect unity, identity – with no longer any forms corresponding to those of the lower worlds. It was a Light!... An almost immaculate white light, yet with something of a golden-rose in it (words are crude). This Light and this Experience were truly wonderful, inexpressible in words.

7th November 1961

You see, Mahalakshmi is the Divine Mother's aspect of love, the perfection of manifested love, which must come before this supreme Love, which is beyond the Manifestation and the Non-manifestation, can be expressed – the supreme Love referred to in Savitri *when the Supreme sends Savitri to the earth:*

For ever love, O beautiful slave of God!
Sri Aurobindo, Savtiri, Book XI

It's to prepare the earth to receive the Supreme's manifestation, the manifestation of His Victory.

11th May 1963

―

And That is... I don't know if this world, I am not talking of the earth alone, but of the present universe, if this world will be followed by others or if it will itself go on, or if... but That, which I am talking about and calling "Love", is the Master of this world.

The day when the earth, because we were promised it, and they aren't vain promises, the day the earth manifests That, it will be a glory.

I've had very faint and momentary perceptions of what it could be – it was beautiful. It was magnificent.

And the physical world is made to express Beauty; if it became harmonious instead of being the ignoble thing it is, if it became harmonious, it would have an exceptional vibratory quality!... It's rather curious: the vital world is magnificent, the mental world has its splendors, the overmental world with all its gods, who are existing beings, I know them well, is truly very beautiful; but I tell you, since I had that Contact, I have

found all that hollow — hollow and... lacking the essential.
And that essential thing, in its principle, is here, on earth.

22nd July 1964

Love is the single, supreme means of manifestation.
And Manifestation automatically implies unfolding. (...)
It's an amused way of looking at religions and all the gods the way you would look at ... they are like theatre performances. They're pastimes; but that's not what can teach you to know yourself, not at all, not at all! You must go right down to the bottom.
And it is this, this descent to the very bottom, in search of... but it isn't an unknown, it isn't an unknown – a bursting, it really is like a bursting, that marvelous bursting of the Vibration of Love; that is... it is the memory. And the effort is to turn it into an active reality.

30th October 1964

(Mother reads a few lines from "Savitri" which she prepares to translate into French. It is Savitri's heart that speaks:)

> The great stars burn with my unceasing fire
> And life and death are both its fuel made.
> Life only was my blind attempt to love:
> Earth saw my struggle, heaven my victory.
> Sri Aurobindo, Savitri, Book X, Canto 3

She says, Life and death are the fuel, *then,* In my blind attempt LIFE ONLY *was my attempt to love.* [Mother later stressed again, "It's not Life was only, but Life only.] *Because my attempt to love was blind, I limited it to life – but I won the victory in death.*

It's very interesting. (Mother repeats:)
Earth saw my struggle, heaven my victory.

Yet, earth should see the victory? The victory should be on earth, shouldn't it?

Yes, but she couldn't win the victory on earth because she lacked heaven – she couldn't win the victory in life because she lacked death and she had to conquer death in order to conquer life.

That's the idea. Unless we conquer Death, the victory isn't won. Death must be vanquished, there must be no more death.

That's very clear.

(silence)

According to what he says here, it is the principle of Love that is transformed into flame and finally into light. It isn't the principle of Light that is transformed into flame when it materializes: it's the flame that is transformed into light.

The great stars give light because they burn; they burn because they are under the effect of Love.

Love would be the original Principle?

That seems to be what he is saying.

I didn't remember this passage. But I told you, my experience [The experience of the "great pulsations" of divine Love (in April, 1962)] *is that the last thing as one rises – the last thing beyond light, beyond consciousness, beyond... – the last thing one reaches is love.*

8th September 1965

You know, you are in considerable discomfort, out of sorts, unable to breathe, you have a feeling of nausea, of helplessness, you can't even move, or think or do anything... in a word, quite out of sorts; and then suddenly... the Consciousness – the bodily consciousness of the Vibration of Love, which is the very essence of the creation, just one second, everything lights up, pfft! Gone, it's all gone. Then you look at yourself, amazed – it's all gone. You were in considerable discomfort – it's all gone.

23rd November 1965

The Pulsations of Love

(After a perilous month, Mother has suddenly had the formidable, decisive experience, and she gives her first message. She is lying on her bed in the room upstairs, and has become quite thin. It is around ten in the morning. Her voice has greatly changed. School children can be heard playing in the distance.)

Night of April 12th - 13th, 1962. [Mother gives the first part of this message in English].

Suddenly in the night I woke up with the full awareness of what we could call the Yoga of the world. The Supreme Love was manifesting through big pulsations, and each pulsation was bringing the world further in its manifestation. It was the formidable pulsations of the eternal, stupendous Love, only Love, each pulsation of the Love was carrying the universe further in its manifestation.

And the certitude that what is to be done is done and the Supramental Manifestation is realized.

Everything was Personal, nothing was individual.

This was going on and on and on and on....

The certitude that what is to be done is DONE.

All the results of the Falsehood had disappeared: Death was an illusion, Sickness was an illusion, Ignorance was an illusion – something that had no reality, no existence.... Only Love, and Love, and Love, and Love – immense, formidable, stupendous, carrying everything.

And how, how to express in the world? It was like an impossibility, because of the contradiction....

But then it came: "You have accepted that this world should know the Supramental Truth... and it will be expressed totally, integrally." Yes, yes....

And the thing is DONE.

13th April 1962

From time to time, one touches the vibration of the Supreme's Love, the creative Love, Love that creates, upholds, maintains, fuels progress and is the Manifestation's very reason for being. These great pulsations were the expression of That, and That is something so stupendous and marvelous for the material frame, the body, that it seems to be dosed out. From time to time, you are given a trickle of it to make you realize that the end or anyway, the end of the beginning! is That.

14th July 1962

So the conclusion, afterwards, naturally, when the whole thing had been seen and studied carefully, the conclusion is that the Lord has neither cause nor effect; and all that is is like those pulsations in my experience two years ago, or a year and a half ago, I don't remember – it was in April, the pulsations of Love bursting forth and creating the world, which followed one another but had neither cause nor effect: one pulsation wasn't the result of the one before or the cause of the one after – not at all – each one was a whole in itself.

Each moment of the Supreme is a whole in itself.

And "moment", what does it mean? What does it correspond to in the truth of the Supreme? I don't know – for us, that's how it is translated, because everything is translated that way for us. All change is translated for us as the sense of time – ONE sense of time, a certain sense of time, which may be infinite and eternal, but is a time all the timeless. What is it? What does it correspond to? I don't know.

22nd January 1964

There was the experience of That, the experience of the great pulsations, but it was an experience... (how can I put it?) of a drop that would be an infinite, or of a second that would be an eternity. While the experience is there, there is absolute certitude; but outwardly, everything starts up again as it was one minute before – That (gesture of pulsation for a second), *puff! Everything is changed; then everything starts up again, with perhaps a slight change that's perceptible only to a consciousness, perceptible to the consciousness, but not concretely perceptible, and with, generally, violent reactions in the Disorder: something that revolts.*

So, to our logic, which is obviously stupid, but anyway, it means that the goal is still very far away, that the world isn't ready.

20th March 1965

I remember, when I came back after having BEEN those bursts – those pulsations, those bursts of creative Love, when I returned to the ordinary consciousness, while retaining the very real memory of That, of the state, well, that state, which I felt to be pulsations of creative Love, is what must, is That which must replace here this consciousness of concrete reality – which is, which becomes unreal, it's like something lifeless – hard, dry, inert, lifeless. And to our ordinary consciousness, I remember how it was in the past, that's what gives you the impression, "This is concrete, this is real. Well, this," this sensation, is what must be replaced by the phenomenon of consciousness of that Pulsation. And That (Mother makes an intense gesture enfolding her whole face) *is at the same time all-light, all-power, all-intensity of love, and such FULLNESS! It's so full that... where That is, nothing else can exist. And when That is here, in the body, in the cells, then all you have to do is focus It on someone or something, and order is instantly restored in the person or the thing.*

So, translated into ordinary words, it "heals". It heals the disease. But it doesn't heal it, it annuls it.... Yes, it annuls it.

12th July 1967

Have you sometimes had that kind of very global vision in time and space, in which each thing takes its own place and everything is coordinated by a total consciousness?... It must be new for me only. It is a knowledge-vision. My consciousness, the consciousness there (gesture above and around) *is constantly a consciousness of action. Since the beginning of those creative bursts of Love, it has been a consciousness of action, always action – action, action, perpetual action. Ultimately, constant creation.*

29th July 1967

Love is the Permanence

Does that mean you're breaking all contacts with the earth?

No, that's not it. Things go on. I don't know, I have no idea. I can't say exactly what it is, but.... It's a.... don't know. In any case, it seems obvious that the NATURE of the contact must become very different. Because in proportion to this detachment, the reality of the Vibration – and especially the vibration of divine Love – keeps growing and growing (out of all proportion to the body, even) in a FORMIDABLE manner, formidable! The body is beginning to feel nothing but that.

Is this detachment necessary, then, for divine Love to be established? I don't know.

Yes, it's as if I were living, as if the BODY were living, despite all the illnesses and attacks, all the ill will besetting it, living in a bath of the divine vibration – bathing in something... immense – immense, immense... limitless, and so stable! The body lives in it like this (gesture as if Mother were floating). *So even when there is what we call physical pain, even when there are blows to morale, like having a cashier ask you for money and you have none to give him, well, despite it all, despite all the possible complications, coming all at the same time, EVERYTHING, everything that happens now, even things which seem extremely unpleasant to our mental conceptions or our mental reactions, everything is a bath, a bath of the vibration of divine Love. So much so that if I didn't control my body, I would be smiling at everything all the time like an idiot. A beatific smile for everything (I don't show it because I control myself).*

27th March 61

We thirst for perfection..., In the experience it was only the BODY, you understand, the other part of the being is quite all right – the body is in this state. All the rest is very happy – very happy, in perpetual joy and eurythmy (gesture of great waves), *feeling divine Love, not Love as such... I don't know how to say it, this Love without object, this Love which is neither 'originated' nor 'received' – without object, without cause or origin. It's the feeling of floating in something.*

16th December 1961

Then, immediately, without transition, it was as if I was plunged in a bath of the Supreme's Love... with the sensation of something limitless; in other words, when you have the perception of space, that something is everywhere, it's beyond the perception of space, but if you have the perception of space, it's everywhere. And it's a kind of homogenous vibratory mass, IMMOBILE, yet with an unparalleled intensity of vibration, which can be described as a warm, golden light, but it's not that, it's much more marvelous than that! And then, it's everywhere at once, everywhere always the same, without alternations of high and low, unchanging, in an unvarying intensity of sensation. And that "something" which is characteristic of divine nature, and is hard to express with words, is at the same time absolute immobility and absolute intensity of vibration. And That... loves. There is no "Lord", there are no "things"; there is no subject, no object. And That loves. But how can you say what That is?... It's impossible. And That loves everywhere and everything, all the time, all at the same time.

All those stories those so-called saints and sages told about God's Love "coming and going", oh, it's unspeakably stupid! – It's THERE, eternally; It has always been there, eternally; It will always be there, eternally, always the same and at the highest of its possibility.

It hasn't left, and now it won't be able to leave.

And once you've lived That... you become so irrevocably conscious that everything depends on the individual perception, entirely; and naturally, that individual perception (of divine Love) *depends on the inadequacy, the inertia, the incomprehension, the incapacity, the cells' inability to hold and keep the Vibration, anyway all that man calls his "character" and which comes from his animal evolution.*

(silence)

It is said that divine Love doesn't manifest because, in the world's present state of imperfection, the result would be a catastrophe – that's a human vision. Divine Love manifests, has manifested eternally, will manifest eternally, and it's the incapacity of the material world... not only of the material world, but of the vital world and the mental world, and of many other worlds that aren't ready, that are incapable – but HE is there, He is there, right there! He is there permanently, it's THE Permanence. The Permanence Buddha sought is there. He claims he found it in Nirvana – it is there, in Love.

22nd July 1964

MISSIONED LOVE

I have had the experience of being 'missioned', so to speak, in a form of Love and Consciousness combined – divine Love in its supreme purity, divine Consciousness in its supreme purity – and emanated DIRECTLY, without passing through all the intermediate states, directly into the nethermost depths of the Inconscient. And there I had the impression of being, or rather of finding a symbolic Being in deep sleep... so veiled that he was almost invisible. Then, at my contact, the veil seemed to be rent and, without his awakening, there was a sort of radiation spreading out.... I can still see my vision....

The way Théon told it, there was first the universal Mother, he didn't call her the universal Mother, but Sri Aurobindo used that name, the universal Mother in charge of creation. For creating she made four emanations: Consciousness or Light; Life; Love or Beatitude and (Mother tries in vain to remember the fourth)... *I must have cerebral anemia today! In India they speak only of three: Sat-Chit-Ananda (Sat is Existence, expressed by Life; Chit is Consciousness, expressed by Power; Ananda is Bliss, synonymous with Love). But according to Théon, there were four (I knew them by heart). Well, these emanations, Théon narrated it in such a way that someone not a philosopher, someone with a childlike mind, could understand), these emanations, conscious of their own power, separated themselves from their Origin; that is, instead of being entirely surrendered to the supreme Will and expressing only.... Ah, the fourth emanation is Truth! Instead of carrying out only the supreme Will, they seem to have acquired a sense of personal power. They were personalities of sorts, universal personalities, each representing a mode of being. Instead of remaining connected, they cut the link – each acted on his own, to put it simply. Then, naturally, Light became darkness, Life became death, Bliss became suffering and Truth became falsehood. And these are the four great Asuras, the Asura of Inconscience, the Asura of Falsehood, the Asura of Suffering and the Asura of Death.*

Once this had occurred, the divine Consciousness turned towards the Supreme and said (Mother laughs): *'Well, here's what has happened. What's to be done?' Then from the Divine came an emanation of Love, in the first emanation it wasn't Love, it was Ananda, Bliss, the Delight of being which became Suffering, and from the Supreme came Love; and Love descended into this domain of Inconscience, the result of the creation of the first emanation, Consciousness – Consciousness and Light had become Inconscience and Darkness. Love descended straight from the Supreme into this Inconscience; the Supreme, that is, created a new emanation, which didn't pass through the intermediate worlds, because, according to the story, the universal Mother first created all the gods who, when they descended, remained in contact with the Supreme and created all the intermediate worlds to counterbalance this fall – it's the old story of the 'Fall,' this fall into the Inconscient. But that wasn't enough. Simultaneously with the creation of the gods, then, came this direct Descent of Love into Matter, without passing through all the intermediate worlds. That's the story of the first Descent.*

28th July 1961

It was like a memory, an eternally present memory of that consciousness of supreme Love emanated by the Lord onto earth – INTO earth – to draw it back again to Him. And truly it was the descent of the very essence of the divine nature into the most total divine negation, and thus the abandonment of the divine condition to take on terrestrial darkness, so as to bring Earth back to the divine state. And unless That, that supreme Love, becomes all-powerfully conscious here on Earth, the return can never be definitive.

21st January 1962

Sri Aurobindo considered Christ an Avatar (a minor form of Avatar). One emanation of the Divine's aspect of Love, he always said.

15th December 1962

(Mother reads to the disciples an excerpt from Sri Aurobindo's THE MOTHER, in which he describes the different aspects of the Creative Power – what is India is called the 'Shakti,' or the 'Mother' – which have presided over universal evolution.)

> ... There are other great Personalities of the Divine Mother, but they were more difficult to bring down and have not stood out in front with so much prominence in the evolution of the earth-spirit. There are among them Presences indispensable for the supramental realization, – most of all one who is her Personality of that mysterious

and powerful ecstasy and Ananda which flows from a supreme divine Love, the Ananda that alone can heal the gulf between the highest heights of the supramental spirit and the lowest abysses of Matter, the Ananda that holds the key of a wonderful divines. Life and even now supports from its secrecies the work of all the other Powers of the universe.

The Mother   *Sri Aurobindo*

(A disciple:) Sweet Mother, what is this Personality and when will It manifest?

My answer is ready...
She has come, bringing with Her a splendor of power and love, an intensity of divine joy heretofore unknown to the Earth. The physical atmosphere has been completely changed by her descent, permeated with new and marvelous possibilities.
But if She is ever to reside and act here, She has to find at least a minimal receptivity, at least one human being with the required vital and physical qualities, a kind of super-Parsifal gifted with an innate and integral purity, yet possessing at

the same time a body strong enough and poised enough to bear unwaveringly the intensity of the Ananda She brings.

Thus far, She has not found what is needed. Men remain obstinately men and do not want to or are unable to become supermen. All they can receive and express is a love at their own dimension: a human love — whereas the supreme bliss of divine Ananda eludes their perception.

At times, finding the world unready to receive Her, She contemplates withdrawing. But how cruel a loss this would be!

It is true that at present, her presence is more rhetorical than factual, since so far She has had no chance to manifest. Yet even so, She is a powerful instrument in the Work, for of all the Mother's aspects, She holds the greatest power to transform the body. Indeed, those cells which can vibrate at the touch of the divine Joy, receive it and bear it, are cells reborn, on their way to becoming immortal.

But the vibrations of divine Bliss and those of pleasure cannot cohabit in the same vital and physical house. We must therefore TOTALLY renounce all feelings of pleasure to be ready to receive the divine Ananda. But rare are those who can renounce pleasure without thereby renouncing all active participation in life or sinking into a stern asceticism.

And among those who realize that the transformation is to be wrought in active life, some pretend that pleasure is a form of Ananda gone more or less astray and legitimize their search for self-satisfaction, thereby creating a virtually insuperable obstacle to their own transformation.

Now, if there is anything else you wish to ask me ... Anyone may ask, anyone – anyone who has something to say – not just the students.

Mother, even if we have not previously succeeded, can't we still try?

What? (the disciple repeats his question) *Oh! You can always try!*

The world is recreated from minute to minute. If you knew how – I mean if you could change your nature – you could recreate a new world this very minute!

I didn't say She HAD gone. I said She was CONTEMPLATING it ... at times, now and then.

But Mother, if She came down, She must have seen a possibility!

She came down because there WAS a possibility – because things had reached such a stage that it was her hour to come down. But in truth, She came down because ... because I thought it was possible for her to succeed.

Possibilities are still there – only they have to materialize.

This is borne out by the fact that her descent took place at a given moment and for two or three weeks the atmosphere – not only of the Ashram but of the Earth – was so highly charged with such a power of such an intense divine Bliss creating so marvelous a force that things difficult to do before could be done almost instantly.

There were repercussions the world over. But I don't believe that a single one of you noticed it ... you cannot even tell me when it happened, can you?

When did it happen?

I don't know dates. I don't know, I never remember dates. I can only tell you this ... that it happened before Sri Aurobindo left his body, that he was told about it beforehand and that he ... well, he acknowledged the fact.

But there was a formidable battle with the Inconscient, for when I saw that the level of receptivity was not what it should have been, I blamed the Inconscient ... and tried to wage the battle there.

I don't say it was ineffectual, but between the result obtained and the result hoped for, there was a considerable difference. But as I said, you who are all so near, so steeped in this atmosphere ... who among you noticed anything? – You simply went on with your little lives as usual.

I think it was in 1946, Mother, because you told us so many things at that time.

Right.

(A child:) Sweet Mother, now that She has come, what should we do?

You don't know?

(silence)

Try to change your consciousness...
   But if a force like Hers could manifest and be received here, it would have INESTIMABLE results! ...

(Mother gets up to go, but while leaving, She says to the children around her)

If you had made just one little decision to try to feel your psychic being, my time would not have been wasted.

25th August 1954

TRUE LOVE

Some time ago I made a discovery of that kind, someone asked me if there was any difference between Ananda and Love; I said, "No." Then he said to me, "But then how is it that some people feel Ananda while others feel Love?..." I answered him, "Yes! Those who feel Ananda are those who like to receive, who have the capacity to receive, and those who feel Love are those who have the capacity to give. But it's the same thing, you receive it as Ananda, you give it as Love.

17th July 1963

(Mother first reads her notation of a recent experience)

It came in English. (I want to put it in the Bulletin to fill a gap!) We should put it in French, too.
 Love is... (no need to say that it's the condensation of an experience — an experience I leave unsaid).

Love is not sexual intercourse. Love is not vital attraction and interchange. Love is not the heart's hunger for affection. Love is a mighty vibration coming straight from the One. And only the very

> *pure and very strong are capable of receiving and manifesting it.*

Then an explanation on what I mean by "pure", the very pure and very strong:

> To be pure is to be open only to the Supreme's influence, and to no other.

Far more difficult than what people consider purity to be! Which is something quite artificial and false.

The last sentence I wrote in French, too (the two came together):

> Être pur, c'est être ouvert seulement a l'influence du Supreme et a nulle autre.

It's simple and definite.

Now we should translate the rest into French — I have so many papers that I am lost! *(Mother rummages among a heap of scraps of paper)* I am snowed under with papers!

At first I put, L'Amour n'a rien a voir avec... [Love has nothing to do with...], and so on, but that's not true. So we'll put, L'Amour n'est pas... [Love is not...].

> L'Amour n'est pas les relations sexuelles. L'Amour n'est pas les attractions et les echanges vitaux.
> L'Amour n'est pas le besoin d'affection du coeur...

It's from Savitri, *in "The Debate of Love and Death", when Death tells Savitri, "What you call love is the hunger of your heart".*

> Could we translate: "L'Amour n'est pas le coeur et son besoin d'affection" [Love is not the heart and its hunger for affection]?

But the heart can manifest Love! No: L'Amour n'est pas le besoin d'affection du coeur [Love is not the heart's hunger for affection]. And then, the positive side:

> L'Amour est une vibration toute-puissante emanee directement de l'Un. Et seul, le tres pur et le tres fort est capable de la recevoir et de la manifester.

25th September 1963

I have been asked a question (Mother looks for a note):

> How can I love the Lord? I have never seen Him and never He speaks to me.

This is my answer:

> It is not what one sees or hears that one loves, it is love that one loves through the forms and sounds, and of all love the most perfect love, the most loving love is the Lord's love.

When I wrote it, it was an extraordinarily intense experience, one cannot love anything but love, and it is love that one loves behind all things – it is love that one loves. It is Love that loves itself everywhere.

And form and sound are excuses.

(silence)

Do you find it hard to understand?

No, because I gave it to N. to read – he just blinked; I gave it to U. to read – he just blinked.... So do ...you... blink, too?

No! I find it...

Oh, good! Then it's all right! If at least one person understands, that's enough.

That's the truth, it IS love.... Others will understand.

I like that. It has a sort of childlike simplicity: "... and the most perfect love, the most loving love is the Lord's love."

10th April 1965

And love, which is unconditioned: it doesn't depend on whether you are loved or not, whether you are intelligent or not, whether you are wicked or not – that goes without saying. But it was put in a ridiculous way. But it goes without saying, love is unconditioned, otherwise it isn't love, it's what I call bargaining: "I give you my affection so you give me yours; I am nice to you so you are nice to me!" That's how people understand it, but it's stupid, it's meaningless. That's something I understood when I was quite small, I used to say, "No! You may wish others to be nice to you if you are nice to them, but that has nothing to do with love, no, nothing, absolutely nothing." The very essence of love is unconditioned.

14th June 1965

Basically, what you are complaining about is that you cannot love.

    Yes, but of course!

It's that you don't know how to love. That you aren't open to Love. But that doesn't depend on anything outside you. It depends only on you.
    When I speak of "seeing", that's what I mean.

Seeing... Seeing, it's not "seeing"! It's not a question of seeing. One may see and not love. That's not the point. It's not a question of seeing. It's a door that's still closed.

You are trying to see because you are still trying to love here (gesture to the forehead). *You don't know about that, but I do. You are trying to love here, and so you speak of seeing. But that's not where one loves. And there's no need to see someone in order to love him. That's not true.*

If I am asked, "Have you seen the Lord?" I can't say humanly that I have seen the Lord. But He is here, oh, yes! He is here and He is perfect love. He is here and He is fantastic power.

And He is here, and He is in fact the very essence of true Love, and without this Vibration, one doesn't know what to love is, one cannot know. And unless one rejects all one's personal egoistic limitations, one cannot love Him.

20th October 1965

You have spoken of Divine Love; but Divine Love, when it touches the physical, does not awaken the gross lower vital propensities; indulgence of them would only repel it and make it withdraw again to the heights from which it is already difficult enough to draw it down into the coarsensess of the material creation which it alone can transform. Seek the Divine Love through the only gate through which it will consent to enter, the gate of the psychic being, and cast away the lower vital error.

Letters on Yoga, III, p. 1,509   Sri Aurobindo

FLOWERS

And this one is a wonder! (Mother gives Divine Love Governing the World - Brownea coccinea) *What strength! It's generous, expansive, without narrowness, pettiness, or limitations – when that comes....*

7th March 1961

This is a time of extremes, even extremes in the downright material. Did I tell you two the other day that I had received the first flower of a plant which visibly was supramental power – a flower like this (gesture), *a hibiscus? And yesterday there was the first flower of another plant, also a hibiscus, this big, snow-white, with such a color at the center! An indefinable color, it can't be described.... It's golden pink, but so beautiful that you wonder how such colors can be physical. A flower this big* (gesture, about five inches), *the first flower was yesterday. And that was VISIBLY (it expressed itself, you know) the Victory of Love, the Power of Love.... It's as if all this physical Nature were, oh, like this* (gesture of intense aspiration), *trying – she tries, and there is a Response. They are blessed not to have a mind.*

It was beautiful. It doesn't keep, otherwise I would have kept it to show it to you. How beautiful it was! Like this (same gesture of fervent aspiration): *a thirst, a thirst for the Divine, a thirst for the Divine. All those mental ratiocinations and complications, it all goes round and round in circles. Yes, it does bring about what's now taking place: a sordid conflict, really sordid, between Falsehood and Truth.*

19th October 1967

Here (Mother gives some flowers), *this is the Generosity of inspiration, and this is the crowning achievement* [Divine Love - Punica granatum, the Pomegranate flower].

18th August 1961

[The pomegranate tree is the symbol of Divine Love; the fruit of the tree has been named by Mother 'Divine Love spreading over the World'.]

8th July 1970

One wonders what it will take to shake all this?
(Mother goes again into a meditation, then gives a start)
There was in my hand a vase containing Divine Love [pomegranate] flowers; I wanted to hand it to you, and when it came above my knees... Did you see that movement?

Yes.

It was the vase falling on my knees. It didn't fall on the floor, it fell here....
What does it mean?

(long silence)

I don't know what it means.

2nd November 1968

―

I wanted to take this little rose ('Tenderness for the Divine'), *for I consider it to be the manifestation nearest to divine Love. It's disinterested, spontaneous, intimate.*
This is what I wanted to take with me to my super-heaven, as the most precious thing in the human heart.

10th August 1956

(Mother gives Satprem a rose.) *This is the Tenderness of the Divine for... for himself! The tenderness He has for his creation. 'Creation'... I don't like that word, as if it all were created from nothing! It is He himself, creating with all his tenderness. Some of these roses get quite big; they're so lovely!*

7th January 1961

(Mother gives Satprem a flower: a rose)
It's beautiful. Far lovelier than human beings.
Oh, yes, that's for sure!

21st August 1965

.... See this (Mother shows a big red rose of a particular type), *it's Sri Aurobindo. Wherever people grow this rose on earth, it's Sri Aurobindo. It grows as big as this.*

25th October 1967

(Mother enters in contemplation and passes then a red rose to Satprem)

This is 'all the human passions turned towards the Divine', and that (Mother gives a rose-coloured rose), *this is the answer.*

4th March 1970

HUMAN LOVE

If human love came forth unalloyed, it would be all-powerful. Unfortunately, in human love, there is as much SELF love as love for the beloved; it is not a love that makes you forget yourself. Evidently the gods of the Puranas are a good deal worse than human beings, as we saw in that film the other day, and that story was absolutely true. The gods of the Overmind are infinitely more egocentric – the only thing that counts for them is their power, the extent of their power. Man has in addition a psychic being, so consequently he has true love and compassion – wherein lies his superiority over the gods.

9th August 1958

---

88 – This world was built by Death that he might live. Wilt thou abolish death? Then life too will perish. Thou canst not abolish death, but thou mayst transform it into a greater living.

89 – This world was built by Cruelty that she might love. Wilt thou abolish cruelty?

Then love too will perish. Thou canst not abolish cruelty, but thou mayst transfigure it into its opposite, into a fierce Love and Delightfulness.

90 – This world was built by Ignorance and Error that they might know. Wilt thou abolish ignorance and error? Then knowledge too will perish. Thou canst not abolish ignorance and error, but thou mayst transmute them into the utter and effulgent exceeding of reason.

91 – If life alone were and not death, there could be no immortality; if love were alone and not cruelty, joy would be only a tepid and ephemeral rapture; if reason were alone and not ignorance, our highest attainment would not exceed a limited rationality and worldly wisdom.

92 – Death transformed becomes Life that is Immortality; Cruelty transfigured becomes

Love that is intolerable ecstasy; Ignorance transmuted becomes Light that leaps beyond wisdom and knowledge.

Aphorims   Sri Aurobindo

It's the same idea, that opposition and opposites stimulate progress. Because to say that without Cruelty, Love would be tepid... The principle of Love, as it is beyond the Manifest and the Non-manifest, has nothing to do with either tepidness or cruelty. But Sri Aurobindo's idea, it seems, is that opposites are the most effective and rapid way to knead Matter so that it may intensify its manifestation.

As an experience, it's absolutely certain: when you come in touch with eternal Love, supreme Love, the first, immediate..., what should I say? perception or sensation, it's not an understanding, it is much more concrete is that even the most enlightened, kneaded, prepared material consciousness is INCAPABLE of manifesting That! The first impression is that sort of incapacity. Then comes the experience of something manifesting a type of... not exactly "cruelty", because it's not cruelty as we conceive it; but in the totality of circumstances, there is a vibration which is felt as a certain intensity of refusal of love as it is manifested here — that's exactly the thing: something in the material world refuses the manifestation of love as it exists at present (I don't refer to the ordinary world but to the consciousness at its present highest). It's an experience, I am speaking of something that has taken place. Then the part of the consciousness that has been touched by that opposition calls out directly to Love's origin WITH AN INTENSITY IT COULD NOT HAVE HAD WITHOUT THE EXPERIENCE OF THE REFUSAL. Limits are broken, a flood descends which could NOT manifest before, and something is expressed which was not expressed before.

That happened not very long ago.

15th May 1963

From my earliest childhood, when I was five, my memories at five, and for more than eighty years, I have always been surrounded with people who brought me an abundance of revolt, discontent, and then, more and more so, cases, certain cases have been very acute and still are, of sheer ingratitude — not towards me, that doesn't matter at all, towards the

Divine. Ingratitude... that is something I have often found very, very painful – that it should exist. It's one of the things I have seen in my life that seemed to me the most... the most intolerable – that sort of acid bitterness against the Divine, because things are as they are, because all that suffering was permitted. It takes on more or less ignorant, more or less intellectual forms... but it's a kind of bitterness. It takes sometimes personal forms, which makes the struggle even more difficult because you can't mix in questions of persons – it's not a personal question, it's an ERROR to think that there can be a single "personal" movement in the world; it's man's ignorant consciousness which makes it personal, but it isn't: it's all terrestrial attitudes.

It came with the Mind; animals don't have that. And that's why I feel a sweetness in animals, even the supposedly most ferocious, which doesn't exist in man.

(long silence)

And yet, of all movements, the one that gives perhaps the most joy – an unalloyed joy, untainted by that egoism – is spontaneous gratitude.

It is something very special. It isn't love, it isn't self-offering....

It's a very FULL joy. Very full.

It is a very special vibration unlike anything other than itself. It is something that widens you, that fills you — that is so fervent! It is certainly, of all the movements within the reach of human consciousness, the one that draws you the most out of your ego. And when it can be a gratitude without motive, that vibration, basically, the vibration of what exists towards the Cause of existence... then a great many barriers vanish instantly.

(Mother contemplates that vibration of gratitude for a long time)

When you can enter that vibration in its purity, you realize immediately that it has the same quality as the vibration of Love: it is directionless. It isn't something going from one thing to another, it doesn't go from here to there (gesture from low to high) *or there to here... it is* (round gesture) *simultaneous and total.*

I mean it isn't something that needs the two poles in order to exist; it doesn't go from one pole to the other or from the other to the one: it's a vibration which in its purity is the same as the vibration of Love, which doesn't go from here to there or from there to here – the two poles of existence. It exists in itself for its own delight of being. And what I am saying spoils it a lot.

Like Love.

Men have repeated ad nauseam that nothing exists without those two poles, that those two poles are the cause of existence and everything revolves around them (Mother shakes her head), *but that's not the way it is. This means that man, in his ordinary outward consciousness, cannot understand anything beyond that. There we are. That we know. But in its essence* (Mother again shakes her head), *Love is not like that.*

Ultimately, gratitude is only a very slightly colored hue of the essential Vibration of Love.

21st December 1963

I saw, almost simultaneously, love as people "practice" it, if we may say so, and feel it, and divine Love in its origin. Both were as if shown to me side by side, and not only were they side by side, but I saw also the difference, it was almost simultaneous, between the two actions, how human action is generated and how divine action is produced or manifests. It came through a series of examples or absolutely concrete experiences, lived one after the other, as if a superior Wisdom had organized a whole set of circumstances, circumstances which in themselves were minor, "unimportant" in order to give me the living example of those two things. It was such a concrete and living whole that I took some notes, very succinct and reduced to the minimum as always, and in English. All that is somewhere around, mixed up with other papers. ...

> *Unlike human love which is for some and not for the others, my love is for the Supreme Lord alone, but as the Supreme Lord is all, my love is for all equally.*
>
> *The Lord's love is equal, constant, all-embracing, immutable, eternal.*

Human love, what people call "love," even at its best, even taking it in its purest essence, is something that goes to one person, but not to another: you love SOME people, sometimes even you love only certain qualities in some people; you love SOME people, and that means it's partial and limited. And even for those who are incapable of hatred there is a number of people and things that they are indifferent to there is no love in most cases. That love is limited, partial and defined. It's unstable, moreover: man, I mean the human being, is unable to feel love in a continuous way, always with the same intensity – at certain times, for a moment, it becomes very intense and powerful, and at other times it grows dim; sometimes, it falls completely asleep. And that's under the best conditions – I am not speaking of all the degradations, I am speaking of the feeling people call "love", which is the feeling closest to true love; that's how it is, partial, limited, unstable and fluctuating. ...

We should use another word; what men call "love" is so many different things, with such different mixtures and such different vibrations that it can't be called "love", it can't be given a single name. So it's better simply to say, "No, this isn't Love", that's all. And keep the word for the True Thing.... The word amour [love] in French has a certain evocative power because, whenever I pronounce it, it makes contact; that's why I'd rather keep it. As for all the rest: no, don't talk of love, it isn't love.

I said and wrote somewhere, "Love is not sexual intercourse. Love is not attraction.... Love is not..." and so on, and in the end I said, "Love is an almighty vibration coming straight from the One...." It was a first perception of That.

But it's a fantastic discovery, in the sense that once you have discovered it, it won't leave you no matter what happens.

22nd July 1964

"In spiritual life, one is always a virgin every time...

I never sent it. It was someone (a Frenchwoman) who had a rather curious experience and wrote to me she had suddenly felt that, in love, she was a virgin when she met me, and that it was with a virgin's love that she came to me. So I answered, because it's true: "... one is always a virgin every time one awakens to a new love, for in each case it is a new part of the being, a new state of being that awakens to divine Love."

I wrote it, but didn't send it.

5th June 1965

Very rare and exceptional are the human beings who can understand and feel divine Love, because divine Love is free of attachment and of the need to please the object loved.

That was a discovery.
   That's why people don't understand; for them, love is so much like this (Mother intertwines the fingers of her two hands) *that they cannot even feel or believe that they love if there isn't an attachment like this* (same gesture). *And necessarily, the consequence of attachment is the will, the desire, the need to please the object of one's love.*
   If you take away the attachment and the need to please, people scratch their heads and wonder if they love. And it's only when you take away those two things that divine Love begins!
   This, mon petit, we'll talk about again, it's a revelation.
   That's why they don't understand and that's why they can't feel it.

8th September 1965

Basically, it's the same for everything. The Vital is a sort of super-theatre giving performances — very alluring, dazzling, deceptive performances — and it's only when you know the True Thing that immediately, instinctively, without reasoning, you discern and say, "No, I don't want that."

And for everything, you know. The one point in human life where it has assumed cardinal importance is love. Vital passions and attractions have almost in every case taken the place of the true feeling, which is tranquil, while that makes you bubble with excitement, it gives you the feeling of something "living".... It's very deceptive. And you can know this, feel it, perceive it clearly only when you know the True Thing; if you have touched true love through the psychic and through divine union, then it [vital love] *appears hollow, thin, empty: an appearance and a drama — more often a tragedy than a comedy.*

23rd November 1965

113 – Hatred is the sign of a secret attraction that is eager to flee from itself and furious to deny its own existence. That too is God's play in His creature.

Aphorisms Sri Aurobindo

It corresponds to a sort of vibration – the vibration received from people who hate. It's a vibration which is, so to say, fundamentally the same as the vibration of love. At its very bottom, there is the same sensation. Although on the surface it's the opposite, it is supported by the same vibration. And we could say that we are just as much the slaves of what we hate as of what we love – maybe even more. It's something that keeps hold of you, that obsesses you and which you cherish; a sensation you cherish, because beneath its violence there is a warmth of attraction as great as that which you feel for what you love. And it seems it's only in the activity of the manifestation, that is to say, quite on the surface, that there is this distorted appearance.

You are obsessed by what you hate still more than by what you love. And the obsession stems from that inner vibration.

All these "feelings" (what can we call them?) have a vibratory mode, with something very essential at their core and kinds of layers covering it; so the most central vibration is identical, and it's as it "inflates" to express itself that it gets distorted. For love it's perfectly obvious; in the vast majority of cases it becomes outwardly something with a wholly different nature from the inner vibration, because it's something turning in on itself, shriveling up and trying to pull to itself in an egoistic movement of possession. You WANT to be loved. You say, "I love this person", but at the same time there is what you want, and the lived feeling is, "I want to be loved". And so that's almost as great a distortion as the distortion of hatred, which consists in wanting to destroy what you love in order not to be tied down. Because you cannot obtain what you want from the object of your love, you want to destroy it in order to be freed; and in the other case, you shrivel up almost in an inner fury because you cannot obtain, you cannot gobble up what you love. (Laughing) *In actual fact, from the standpoint of the deeper truth, there isn't much difference!*

It's only when the central vibration remains pure and is expressed in its original purity, which is a spreading out, what can I call it?... It's something radiating out, a vibration spreading out in a glory, a vibration blossoming out, yes, a radiant blossoming out, then it remains true. And materially it's expressed by self-giving, self-forgetfulness, the generosity of the soul. And that's the only true movement. But what people are used to calling "love" is as removed from the central vibration of true Love as hatred; only, the one turns in on itself, shrivels up and hardens, while the other strikes – that's what makes the whole difference. And this isn't seen with ideas: it's seen with vibrations. It's very interesting.

In fact, I've had to study this quite a bit lately! I've had the opportunity to see these vibrations, the outward results may be deplorable, from a practical viewpoint they may be detestable, meaning that this sort of vibration [of hatred] *encourages the need to harm, to destroy; but from the standpoint of the deeper truth, it's not a much greater distortion than the other* ["love"], *it's just of a more aggressive nature – hardly even that.*

But if you follow the experience farther and deeper, if you concentrate on this vibration, you realize it is the original Vibration of the creation and that this Vibration is what has been transformed, distorted in everything that is. So then, there is a sort of understanding warmth, we can't exactly call it "sweetness", but it's a sweetness that would be strong, an understanding warmth in which there is as much smile as sorrow – much more smile than sorrow.... It's not to legitimize the distortion, but it's mostly a reaction against the choice that human mentality, and especially human morality, has made between one particular type of distortion and another. There is a whole series of distortions that have been labeled "bad" and there is a whole series of distortions towards which people are full of leniency, almost compliments. And yet, from the essential standpoint, this distortion is hardly better than that distortion – it's a question of choice.

Ultimately, what's necessary would be first to perceive THE central Vibration, then to appreciate its UNIQUE and marvelous quality to such a point that you automatically and spontaneously move away from all distortions, whether virtuous distortions or evil distortions.

We always come back to the same thing, there is only one solution: to reach the truth of things and cling to it – that essential truth, the truth of essential Love, and cling to it.

25th December 1965

But I never said Auroville was the city of love, never, not once!
The word is too subject to misuse. It would be better not to talk about it.

In fact, the word "love" can be used only with the word "divine" before it. It's the only way it can be used. Without the word "divine", it becomes impossible. And these people refuse to use the word "divine."

   Yes, they're afraid of it. ...

   It's troublesome

(Mother remains silent for a while) *Should I send her this:*

   "Beware of the word 'love' if it is not preceded by the adjective 'divine', because in the general mentality the word evokes sexuality."

17th February 1968

Only the opinion of the Supreme Lord is important. Only the Supreme Lord deserves all our love and returns it hundredfold.

11th February 1970

THE DIRECT TRANSFORMING POWER

But if we want to know or understand the nature of the Force or Power that permits and accomplishes this transformation, specially in the case of evil, but for ugliness to some extent as well, we see that of all powers, Love is obviously the mightiest, the most integral – integral in that it applies to all cases. It's even mightier than the power of purification which dissolves bad wills and is, in a way, master over the adverse forces, but which doesn't have the direct transforming power; because the power of purification must FIRST dissolve in order to form again later. It destroys one form to make a better one from it, while Love doesn't need to dissolve in order to transform, it has the direct transforming power. Love is like a flame changing the hard into the malleable, then sublimating even the malleable into a kind of purified vapor. It doesn't destroy, it transforms.

Love, in its essence and in its origin, is like a white flame obliterating ALL resistances. You can have the experience yourself, whatever the difficulty in your being, whatever the weight of accumulated mistakes, the ignorance, incapacity, bad will, a single SECOND of this Love – pure, essential, supreme – melts everything in its almighty flame. One single moment and an entire past can vanish. One single TOUCH of That in its essence and the whole burden is consumed.

It's easy to understand how someone who has this experience can spread it and act upon others, since to have it you must touch the unique, supreme Essence of the whole manifestation – the Origin and the Essence, the Source and the Reality of all that is; then you immediately enter the realm of Unity where there is no more separation among individuals, it's a single vibration that can repeat itself endlessly in outer forms.

10th January 1961

And it corresponds to a state where you are so PERFECTLY identified with all that is, that you concretely become all that is antidivine – and so you can offer it up. It can be offered up and really transformed through this offering.

This sort of will in people for purity, for Good, which in ordinary mentality is expressed by a need to be virtuous, is actually the GREAT OBSTACLE to true self-giving. It's the root of Falsehood, the very source of hypocrisy, the refusal to take up one's share of the burden of difficulties. And that's what Sri Aurobindo has touched on in this aphorism, directly and very simply.

Do not try to be virtuous. See to what extent you are united, ONE with all that is antidivine. Take up your share of the burden; accept to be impure and false yourself, and in so doing you will be able to take up the Shadow and offer it. And insofar as you are able to take it and offer it, things will change. When Satprem published extracts from this conversation in the Ashram Bulletin of April 1962, Mother had this passage modified, over his protests. Instead of *"Do not try to be virtuous,"* she put *"Do not try to seem virtuous"*; and she added: *"There's a drawback here. People never understand anything, or rather they understand everything in their own way. They would take this sentence as an encouragement to get into mischief, to misbehave, to entertain wrong feelings, and then proclaim, 'We are the Lord's favorites!'... There was something like it in one of Sri Aurobindo's letters, you remember – a letter to people who wanted to bring all the impurities in themselves out to the surface; he told them that was definitely not the way!"*

Don't try to be among the pure. Accept to be with those who are in darkness and, in total love, offer it all.

21st January 1962

I don't know, maybe for others it [the ecstasy] is allowed to last, but for this body... After a while, all the problems from outside come back, that is to say, all the vibratory difficulties of the world are allowed to reach it again in order to be taken up and transformed in the Light of the Lord. And the whole problem crops up again.

You know, problems of illness, problems of possession, vital and mental possession, problems of egos that refuse to yield and this results in circumstances which, humanly, are described in the ordinary way: such and such a thing has happened to so-and-so — but that's not how it comes into the consciousness, well, if you look at things in a sufficiently general way, those problems REMAIN problems. There is indeed something, but a "something" that is still elusive, elusive in its essence: it has to do with feeling, with sensation, with perception, also with aspiration — it has to do with all that, and it is... what we habitually call divine Love, that is, essential Love, that which is expressed by Love and seems to be beyond the Manifestation and Non-manifestation, which, naturally, becomes Love in the Manifestation. And That would be the ALL-POWERFUL expression. In other words, That is what would have the power to transform into divine consciousness and substance all the chaos we now call "world." ...

I have a very strong feeling that it's only That, only with That that things can change, all the rest is inadequate.

20th March 1965

It seems that the only method capable of overcoming all resistances is the method of Love; but in fact, the adverse forces have perverted it in such a way that a large quantity of sincere people, of sincere seekers, seem to be armor-plated against this method, because of its distortion. That's the difficulty. That's why it takes time. Anyway...

29th May 1965

Well, I don't think words can convey this. It's not even a question of living in the atmosphere — what is it?... Maybe one day it will be a power. The power to pass this on. Then it will be possible for everything to change.

Probably when it's there, permanently established.

When it must be, it will be, no?

23rd November 1965

Truth does not depend on any external form and shall manifest in spite of all bad will or opposition.

I've written this in answer to this gentleman [Death]. It came with a power: "Ah, you shall see".

But I'd like to know what Savitri says. What does Savitri say?...

There's no time left, we'll see that next time.

What does she say to him? I think she always says the same thing: the omnipotence of Love.

There you feel the Force. Otherwise it wouldn't be worth living – it really isn't worth it, it's no fun.

19th February 1966

Over and over, I keep saying one thing: "To divine Love, all human confusions and misunderstandings are unknown." There. Well, we will see. "Wherever divine Love is present, human confusions and misunderstandings cannot exist, cannot enter."

That's the only solution.

But not an ATOM of mind must be added – the slightest intellectual activity spoils everything.

And then look at it all with a crystalline smile.

12th July 1962

First Truth then Love

To bring the Divine Love and Beauty and Ananda into the world is, indeed, the whole crown and essence of our yoga. But it has always seemed to me impossible unless there comes as its support and foundation and guard the Divine Truth – what I call the supramental and its Divine Power...

Letters on Yoga, II, p.753 Sri Aurobindo

Here it's clear: he says that what he calls the "Supramental" is the Divine Truth, and that it must come first, and the rest comes afterwards.
...But Sri Aurobindo says that Truth should be established first, and that what he calls the Supramental is the supreme Truth, the Divine Truth. It corresponds to what I noticed while translating that last chapter on "the perfection of the being" in the "Yoga of Self-Perfection": I kept thinking, "But that's only the aspect of Truth; all that he expresses is the aspect of Truth; always and everywhere, it's the angle of Truth; and his supramental action is an action of Truth."

I didn't know he had said it, but it's written clearly here:
> ... But it has always seemed to me impossible unless there comes as its ·support and foundation and guard the Divine Truth - what I call the supramental - and its Divine Power. Otherwise Love itself blinded by the confusions of this present consciousness may stumble in its human receptacles and, even otherwise, may find itself unrecognised, rejected or rapidly degenerating and lost in the frailty of man's inferior nature. But when it comes in the divine truth and power, Divine Love descends first as something transcendent and universal and out of that transcendence and universality it applies itself to persons according to the Divine Truth and Will, creating a vaster, greater, purer personal love than any the human mind or heart can now imagine. It is when one has felt this descent that one can be really an instrument for the birth and action of the Divine Love in the world.
>
> *Letters on Yoga, II, p. 753*   Sri Aurobindo

If divine Love were to descend first, before divine Truth, certain beings with a special power or receptivity might draw it into themselves, personally, and then all those wrong impulses might occur. ["Otherwise Love itself blinded by the confusions of this present consciousness may stumble in its human receptacles and, even otherwise, may find itself unrecognised, rejected or rapidly degenerating and lost in the frailty of man's inferior nature."] *But if this divine Love descends only in the Truth, in the Truth-Consciousness, it will enter someone only if that person is ready to receive it. Without a preparation of Truth, there might occur a very powerful attraction of elements unable to keep that Love in its purity; whereas if the preparation of Truth has been done, with that preparation, It will CHOOSE, in order to manifest, the persons, the individualities, who are ready.*

3rd October 1963

More and more, there is something that presses to make itself known and is formulated like this: what wants to come for next February [On February 29th, 1964, second anniversary of the Supramental Manifestation upon earth.] *is the Truth-Light ...*

(Mother repeats like an incantation) *the Truth-Light, the Truth-Force, the Truth-Light, the Truth-Force... to prepare the way for the manifestation of supreme Love.*

But that is for later on.

But immediate, immediate: the Truth-Light, the Truth-Force. It's becoming precise.

I didn't think about it. It was perfectly blank in my head. I didn't know at all. And then that came.

15th January 1964

And if I remember right, Sri Aurobindo said that this manifestation (which he too calls Love) would take place AFTER the supramental manifestation, didn't he?

First Truth, then Love

Then Love.

Yes, he said there were different "levels" in the Supramental – but that (smiling) *is the sauce that makes things more easily digestible! Everyone says things in the way he finds the easiest to assimilate.*

But the experience — the experience — is always beyond words, always.

20th March 1965

There is something apparently paradoxical, but it's very interesting. It's this (Mother takes a piece of paper and writes):

> "The best way to prepare oneself to receive Divine Love is to adhere integrally to the Truth."
>
> (Mother then writes a second note:)
>
> "Adhere totally to the Truth and you will be ready to receive Divine Love."

When you say that to intelligent good folks, their heads spin!... (Mother laughs) *I must say that making their heads spin is great fun for me!*

But the best part is that it's true! It's true, it is like that. Every time that there is (it's more than an aspiration, much more than a will, in English they call it an urge) a thirst to let

Divine Love express itself completely, totally everywhere, the base, the favorable ground is the Truth.

Sri Aurobindo said it, of course. He said it, he wrote it in black and white, I forget the exact words): "The pure divine love can manifest safely only in a... in a ground" (it's not ground... "of Truth." I don't remember now. If we wanted to put it poetically, we'd say, "in a land of Truth."

So before we can proclaim, "Love, manifest yourself, win the Victory," the ground for Truth must be made ready.

16th December 1967

Then, did I tell you about the message for February 21st, 1968 [when Mother will be ninety]? No? Wasn't it with you that it came?...

It's meant to break formulas, you know, thought formulas, mental categories, and it's not my fault, I mean I didn't do it deliberately. It came like that (Mother reads her message):

"The best way to hasten the manifestation of the

Divine's Love is to collaborate for the triumph of the Truth."

So to the superficial mind... As for us, we know it's true because, as Sri Aurobindo said, the Truth has to be truly established and reign for Divine Love to be able to manifest in all its power and glory without... without demolishing everything. Sri Aurobindo put it more strongly than that, he said it would "shatter" everything.
   So that's the message I am going to give.

20th December 1967

The Moment Has Come

It came after the vision of the great divine Becoming. [See conversation of January 12, 1962] *"Since this world is progressive," I was wondering, "since it is increasingly becoming the Divine, won't there always be this deeply painful sense of the non-divine, of the state that, compared with the one to come, is not divine? Won't there always be what we call 'adverse forces', in other words, things that don't harmoniously follow the movement?" Then came the answer, the vision of That: "No, the moment of this very Possibility is drawing near, the moment for the manifestation of the essence of perfect Love, which can transform this unconsciousness, this ignorance and this ill will that goes with it into a luminous and joyous progression, wholly progressive, wholly comprehensive, thirsting for perfection."*

It was very concrete. ...

Most likely the experience could take place only because the time had come for all this to be offered up.

The point is not to perpetuate those things, but to offer them up.

Because the time has come to manifest this Power, which is a power of Love – of LOVE, not merely of identity – of Love, of perfect Love; for perfect Love alone can offer.

It happened this morning, with great simplicity, but at the same time it had something so vast and almighty in it, as if the Universal Mother were turning towards the Lord and saying, "At last! We are ready."

That was my experience this morning.
21st January 1962

Here it's clear: he says that what he calls the "Supramental" is the Divine Truth, *and that it must come first, and the rest comes afterwards.*

And yet, for some time now and increasingly, there has been an extremely concrete Response to a kind of aspiration (a call or prayer) in which I say to the Lord, "Supreme Lord, manifest Your Love." It comes at the end of a long invocation in which I ask Him to manifest all His aspects one after another, one after another, and it ends like that. But then, remarkably enough, at that moment there comes a Response which is growing clearer and clearer, stronger and stronger....
24th July 1963

Then Mother comments again on Sri Aurobindo's second letter:

And were Love to manifest before Truth, there would be catastrophes.

It's curious, for a very long time, for months and almost years, something always stopped me when I asked for Love's manifestation, a sort of very clear impression: "No, it isn't time yet, it isn't time yet...." Until suddenly one day it started off and there came an overwhelming Response. That was several months ago, and ever since then there has been a Response – an ever-increasing Response.

Yet I can't say in all sincerity that the Truth has manifested!

Perhaps the preparation is sufficient?

Perhaps it's an individual question – yet my action isn't individual, there's a constant perception of the earth's atmosphere.

Never mind, to say so gives some comfort!

24th July 1963

I told you about the meeting with Durga. Now there is Kali, waiting. And naturally, it's the great power – the great power, a power... you understand, they are stronger, more powerful than this teeming humanity, so if you let them loose... As for me, I want Love to be victorious RIGHT NOW – she will have the victory, she will, but... not after so much breakage.

19th October 1967

Preparation Is Needed

Sri Aurobindo had also written to the effect, 'If Divine Love were to manifest now in all its fullness and totality, not a single material organism would but burst.' *So we must learn to widen, widen, widen not only the inner consciousness (that is relatively easy – at least feasible), but even this conglomeration of cells. And I've experienced this: you have to be able to widen this sort of crystallization if you want to be able to hold this Force. I know. Two or three times, upstairs (in Mother's room), I felt the body about to burst. Actually, I was on the verge of saying, 'burst and be done with'. But Sri Aurobindo always intervened – all three times he intervened in an entirely tangible, living and concrete way ... and he arranged everything so that I was forced to wait. Then weeks go by, sometimes even months, between one thing and another, so that some elasticity may come into these stupid cells.*

So much time is wasted. We are ... oh! We are so hard! (Mother hits her body) *As hard as a rock.*

11th December 1960

But as it's all-powerful, a certain receptivity must be prepared on earth so its effects are not devastating. Sri Aurobindo has explained it in one of his letters. Someone asked him, 'Why doesn't this Love come now?', and he replied something like this: If divine Love in its essence were to manifest on earth, it would be like an explosion; for the earth is not supple enough or receptive enough to widen to the measure of this Love. The earth must not only open itself but become wide and supple. Matter – not just physical Matter, but the substance of the physical consciousness as well – is still much too rigid.

10th January 1961

And if I tell that to people, they go wide-eyed. It makes no sense to them – to even have the idea of a perfection existing somewhere, an attainable perfection, is already quite a lot for them! So I wrote:

> *We thirst for perfection, not this human perfection which is the perfection of the ego and bars the way to the divine Perfection, but that ONE perfection which has the power to manifest upon Earth the eternal Truth.*

4th July 1962

But you mustn't rush; and above all, no desire. Be very calm. The calmer you are, the longer it lasts. If you're in too much of a hurry, it goes away.

I can see it takes an EXTRAORDINARY capacity and solidity to bear That without exploding – and this capacity is slowly being prepared.

We mustn't be in a hurry.

14th July 1962

And I must say that the state of consciousness that rapture gives would be dangerous in the present state of the world.... Because it has almost absolute reactions – I can see that that state of rapture has an OVERWHELMING power. But I insist on the word "overwhelming", in the sense that it's intolerant of, or intolerable to (yes, intolerable to) all that's unlike it! It's the same thing, or almost (not quite the same but almost), as supreme divine Love: the vibration of that ecstasy or rapture is a first hint of the vibration of divine Love, and that's absolutely... yes, there is no other word, intolerant, in the sense that it doesn't brook the presence of anything contrary to it.

So that would have frightening results for the ordinary consciousness. I can see that very well, because at times that Power comes – the Power comes... and you feel as if everything is about to explode. Because it can tolerate only union, it can tolerate only an accepting response – receiving and accepting. And not from any arbitrary will: from the VERY FACT of its existence, an all-powerful existence – "all-powerful" not in the way man understands all powerfulness: really an all-powerfulness. That is, entirely, totally and exclusively existing. It contains everything, but what is contrary to its vibration is forced to change, you see, since nothing can disappear; but then that immediate, brutal, so to say, and absolute change is, in the world as it is, a catastrophe.

24th August 1963

As soon as I have one minute to meditate, that is to say, as soon as I am not assailed from every side by people, things, events, as soon as I can simply do this (gesture of drawing within) and look, well, I see that the cells themselves are beginning to learn the Vibration. [...]

And I said that that sort of "rain of Truth-Light" which came a few months ago announced something – it has obviously prepared, started this kind of permeation of a superior Harmony into the material vibrations. It has prepared not a "new descent," but the possibility of a new perception, a perception that allows an outward and physical action.

22nd July 1964

Since that experience came, there has no longer even been in the consciousness that sort of care I took for years not to concentrate too much Force or Power, or Light or Love, on beings and things for fear of upsetting their natural growth – that seems so childish! It's there, it's there, it's there – it is there. And it's for things themselves that it's impossible to feel more of it than they can bear.

22nd July 1964

It's an experience I have more and more clearly for the contact with that true divine Love to be able to manifest, that is, to express itself freely, it requires a POWER in beings and in things... which doesn't exist yet. Otherwise, everything breaks apart.

There are scores of very convincing details, but, naturally, as they are "details" or very personal things, I can't talk about them.

But on the basis of the proof or proofs of repeated experiences, I am forced to say this: when that Power of PURE Love – a wonderful Power, beyond any expression – as soon as it begins to manifest fully, freely, a great many things seem to collapse instantly: they can't hold on. They can't hold on, they're dissolved. Then... then everything comes to a stop. And that stop, which we might believe to be a disgrace, is on the contrary an infinite Grace!

Just the ever so slightly concrete and tangible perception of the difference between the vibration in which we live normally and almost continuously and that Vibration, just the realization of that infirmity, which I call nauseous – it really gives you a feeling of nausea – is enough to stop everything.

No later than yesterday, this morning... there are long moments when that Power manifests, and then, suddenly, there is a Wisdom – an immeasurable Wisdom – which makes everything relax in a perfect tranquillity: What is to be will be, it will take the time it will take. Then, everything is fine. With this, everything is immediately fine. But the Splendor goes.

We can only be patient.

16th September 1964

EVERYTHING WILL YIELD

What can make them yield?

Divine Love.
It's the only thing.
Sri Aurobindo has explained it in Savitri.
Only when Divine Love has manifested in all its purity will everything yield, will it all yield — it will then be done.
It's the only thing that can do it.
It will be the great Victory.

(silence)

On a small scale, in very small details, I feel that of all the forces, this is the strongest. And it's the only one with a power over hostile wills. Only ... for the world to change, it must manifest here in all its fullness. We have to be up to it...
11th December 1960

And when the day comes for the manifestation of supreme Love – a crystallized, concentrated descent of supreme Love – that will truly be the hour of Transformation, for nothing will be able to resist That.

10th January 1961

―

But it's clear that in my consciousness the [supreme] contact has been made (with some degree of limitation, but still it has been made), and nothing takes place – nothing, absolutely nothing, not even the most totally in-sig-ni-fi-cant things – without, I can't even say the "thought" or the "sensation" in English they say awareness, *but it's much fuller than that, the feeling (another impossible word), without the feeling of the Lord's Presence, the supreme Presence, being there twenty-four hours a day. Throughout that activity of the night I've just told you about, He was there, the Lord's Presence was there all the time, every second, directing everything, organizing everything – BUT THAT WASN'T THERE. And That, which I call Love, that Manifestation, is so formidably powerful that, as I once said, it is intolerant of anything else – That alone exists....*

That exists, That is – and it's finished. Whereas the Lord (the "Lord," what I call the Lord) is something else altogether; the Lord is all that has manifested, all that hasn't manifested, all that is, all that will be, and all, all is the Lord – it's the Lord. But the Lord (laughing) *is necessarily tolerant of Himself!...*

All is the Lord, but all is perceived by the Lord through the limitations of human perception! But everything, everything is there – everything is there; everything, as it is every second; and with the perception of time, every second is different, in a perpetual becoming. This is supreme Tolerance: there is no more struggle, no more battle, no more destruction – there is only He.

Those who have had this experience have generally stopped there. And if they wanted to get out of the world, they chose the Lord's "aspect of annihilation"; they took refuge there and stayed there – all the rest no longer existed. But the other aspect... the other aspect is the world of tomorrow, or of the day after tomorrow. The other aspect is an inexpressible glory. So all-powerful a glory that it alone exists.

It's ONE way of being of the Lord.

(silence)

This experience is a milestone on the road.
                                    16th September 1964

"One", this "one" is... it's the "I" – I don't know. According to the experience, it's the last thing to manifest now in its purity, and it is the one that has the transforming power. That's what he appears to be saying here: the victory of Love seems to be the final victory.
                                    8th September 1965

Love leads us from the suffering of division into the bliss of perfect union, but without losing that joy of the act of union which is the soul's greatest discovery and for which the life of the cosmos is a long preparation. Therefore to approach God by love is to prepare oneself for the greatest possible spiritual fulfillment.

The Synthesis of Yoga, p. 523   Sri Aurobindo

International Publications

Auroville Architecture
by Franz Fassbender

Auroville Form Style and Design
by Franz Fassbender

Landscapes and Gardens of Auroville
by Franz Fassbender

Inauguration of Auroville
by Franz Fassbender

Auroville in a Nutshell
by Tim Wrey

Death doesn't exist
The Mother on Death, Sri Aurobindo on Rebirth
Compiled by Franz Fassbender

Divine Love
Compiled by Franz Fassbender

Five Dream
by Sri Aurobindo

A Vision
Compiled by Franz Fassbender

Passage to More than India
by Dick Batstone

The Mother on Japan
Compiled by Franz Fassbender

Children of Change: A Spiritual Pilgrimage
by Amrit (Howard Shoji Iriyama)

Memories of Auroville - told by early Aurovilians
by Janet Feran

The Journeying Years
by Dianna Bowler

Auroville Reflected
by Bindu Mohanty

Finding the Psychic Being
by Loretta Shartsis

The Teachings of Flowers
The Life and Work of the Mother of the Sri Aurobindo Ashram
by Loretta Shartsis

The Supramental Transformation
by Loretta Shartsis

The Mother's Yoga - 1956-1973 (English & French)
Vol. 1, 1956-1967 & Vol. 2, 1968-1973
by Loretta Shartsis

Antithesis of Yoga
by Jocelyn Janaka

Bougainvilleas PROTECTION
by Narad (Richard Eggenberger), Nilisha Mehta

Crossroad The New Humanity
by Paulette Hadnagy

Die Praxis Des Integralen Yoga
by M. P. Pandit

The Way of the Sunlit Path
by William Sullivan

Wildlife great and small of India's Coromandel
by Tim Wrey

A New Education With A Soul
by Marguerite Smithwhite

Featured Titles

Divine Love

The texts presented in this book are selected from the Mother and Sri Aurobindo.
"Awakened to the meaning of my heart. That to feel love and oneness is to live. And this the magic of our golden change, is all the truth I know or seek, O sage."

Sri Aurobindo, Savitri, Book XII, Epilog

A Vision by the Mother

On 28th May 1958, the Mother recounted a vision she once had of a wonderful Being of Love and Consciousness, emanated from the Supreme Origin and projected directly into the Inconscient so that the creation would gradually awaken to the Supramental Consciousness. The Mother's account of this vision was brought out a first time in November 1906, in the Revue Cosmique, a monthly review published in Paris.

A Dream – Aims and Ideals of Auroville
the Mother on Auroville

50 years of Auroville from 28.02.1968 - 28.02.2018
Today, information about Auroville is abundant. Many people try to make meaning out of Auroville – about its conception, to what direction should we grow towards, and, what are we doing here?

But what was Mother's original Dream and what was her Vision for Auroville back then?

Matrimandir Talks by the Mother

This book presents most of Mother's Matrimandir talks, including how she conceived the idea for this special concentration and meditation building in Auroville.

Memories of Auroville - Told by early Aurovilians

Memories of Auroville is a book about the very early days of Auroville based on interviews made in 1997 with Aurovilians who lived here between 1968 and 1973. The interviews presented in this book are part of a history program for newcomers that I had created with my friend, Philip Melville in 1997. The plan was to divide Auroville's history into different eras and then interview Aurovilians according to their area of knowledge. Our first section would cover the years from 1968 till 1973 when the Mother was still in her physical body.

The Way of the Sunlit Path

May The Way of the Sunlit Path be a convenient guide for activating this ancient truth as a support for a Conscious Evolution.
May it illumine the transformation offered to us in the Integral Yoga.

A Dream Takes Shape (in English, French, Hindi)

A comprehensive brochure on the international township of Auroville in, ranging from its Charter and "Why Auroville?" to the plan of the township, the central Matrimandir, the national pavilions and residences, to working groups, the economy, making visits, how to join, its relationship to the Sri Aurobindo Ashram, and its key role in the future of the world. This brochure endeavours to highlight how The Mother envisioned Auroville from its inception, some of the major achievements realised over the years, and some of the currently faced in implementing the guidelines which she gave.

Mother on Japan

I had everything to learn in Japan. For four years, from an artistic point of view, I lived from wonder to wonder. And everything in this city, in this country, from beginning to end, gives you the impression of impermanence, of the unexpected, the exceptional... ...everything in this city, in this country, from beginning to end, gives you the impression of impermanence, of the unexpected, the exceptional. You always come to things you did not expect, you want to find them again and they are lost – they have made something else which is equally charming.

Auroville Reflected

On 28 February 1968, on an impoverished plateau on the Coromandel Coast of South India, about 4,000 people from around the world gathered for a most unusual inauguration. Handfuls of soil from the countries of the world were mixed together as a symbol of human unity. Why did Indira Gandhi, the erstwhile Prime Minister of India, support this development for "a city the earth needs?" Why did UNESCO endorse this project? Why does the Dalai Lama continue to be involved in the project? What led anthropologist Margaret Mead to insist that records must be kept of its progress? Why did both historian William Irwin Thompson and United Nations representative Robert Muller note that this social experiment may be a breakthrough for humanity even as critics commented, "it is an impossible dream"?

A House For the Third Millennium
Essays on Matrimandir

Nightwatch at the Matrimandir...
A cosmic spectacle; the black expanse above, the big black crater of Matrimandir's excavation carved deep into the soil. The four pillars - two of which are completed and the other two nearing completion - are four huge ships coming together from the four corners of the earth to meet at this pro propitious spot...

Passage to More than India

This book is a voyage of discovery. In 1959 the author, Dick Batstone, a classically educated bookseller in England, with a Christian background, comes across a life of the great Indian polymath Sri Aurobindo, though a series of apparently fortuitous circumstances. A meeting in Durham, England, leads him to a determination to get to the Sri Aurobindo Ashram in Pondicherry, a former French territory south of Madras.

www.ingramcontent.com/pod-product-compliance
Lightning Source LLC
LaVergne TN
LVHW081543070526
838199LV00057B/3756